THE HAWTHORN SERIES

Perfect

PASTA

Easy-to-prepare inexpensive meals of home-
made or prepared pasta with a host of
delicious sauces.

MURDOCH BOOKS

Sydney • London

—MAKING PASTA—

Pasta comes in a great variety of shapes and sizes

asta and noodles
have been enjoyed in
ny forms throughout
rope and Asia for
turies.
Versatile, quick and
y to prepare, they are
o inexpensive. Served
ply with butter and
ese or dressed with
most elaborate
ce, pasta can be right
any occasion.
The recipes included
this book mainly use
ed pasta, which is
th quick and
nvenient. For a
icious change, try
stituting fresh pasta.

HE DOUGH

sta dough is simple to
pare. Different
vours and textures
be achieved by
ering the basic
gredients just a little.
Pasta dough should
ve a rather dry texture
d be quite firm. If the
ugh becomes too
ist, it is difficult to

work with, so knead in a
little extra flour to
achieve the right
consistency.

Kneading is essential
to make the dough
elastic and easy to
handle. Check after
5–10 minutes — dough
is sufficiently kneaded
when you make a light
indentation in it with
your finger and the
dough springs back
immediately. At this
stage dough is too elastic
to roll, so wrap in plastic
wrap or waxed paper
and leave for about 10
minutes — the dough
will soften slightly and
be easier to roll out.

Fresh Pasta Dough

Preparation time:
  10 minutes
Cooking time: nil

3 cups plain flour
3 eggs
1 tablespoon olive oil
3 tablespoons water

1 Sift flour into a large
bowl or into a mound on
a flat surface. Make a
well in the centre. Whisk
together eggs, oil and
water.
2 Add three-quarters of
the egg mixture to the
flour and cut liquid
through flour using two
flat-bladed knives. Add
remaining liquid if
needed, to form a stiff
dough. Knead dough for
about 20 minutes until
smooth and elastic.
Divide dough into four
pieces and use as
desired.

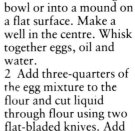

HINT
Freeze prepared fresh
pasta in freezer bags
or foil for up to three
months. Cook
directly from the
frozen state.

aking pasta

Sift flour onto a flat
rface. Add egg, oil
d water.

2 Mix dough using two
flat-bladed knives.

3 Knead dough until
smooth and elastic.

Pasta varieties, from left to right: Chickpea and Garlic, Cheese and Basil, Lemon and Pepper, Spinach, Almond, Saffron, Buckwheat, Tomato and Wholemeal Pastas

Fresh Semolina Pasta

Preparation time:
  10 minutes
Cooking time: nil

3 cups fine semolina
2 eggs
1 tablespoon olive oil
200 mL lukewarm water

1 Sift semolina into a large bowl or into a mound on a flat surface. Make a well in the centre. Whisk together eggs, oil and water.
2 Add three-quarters of the egg mixture to the semolina and cut liquid through semolina using two flat-bladed knives. Add remaining liquid if needed, to form a stiff dough. Knead dough for about 10 minutes until smooth and elastic. Divide dough into four pieces. Roll and shape as desired.

ROLLING PASTA

Pasta can be rolled by hand, which takes a little time, but for the inexperienced cook is easily managed if the pasta is rolled in small lots.

Using a pasta machin[e] makes rolling the pasta far easier and if you ha[ve] a passion for fresh past[a] it is a worthwhile investment.

Rolling by Hand
Take a quarter of the dough and place it on a clean, flat, lightly floured work surface, such as a kitchen bench or table. Flatten the dough lightly with the palm of your hand.
  Use a large rolling pi[n] and roll pasta out thin[ly] rolling from the centre [to] the edge. Avoid rolling over the edge since this makes the edges paper

4

1 and harder to
ndle. Keep moving
led dough and dust
ard and rolling pin
h extra flour if
ded. After rolling,
and shape as desired.
he pasta is not being
or shaped
mediately, cover with
ean dry tea-towel
h a damp tea-towel
top. This prevents
ugh drying out and
oming brittle.

lling by Machine
vide dough into four

pieces, and flatten lightly
on a floured board.

Set the roller on the
pasta machine to the
widest setting and dust
with a little flour.

Feed each portion of
dough through the
machine twice. Lay flat
on a board and fold into
three. Feed the folded
pastry, unfolded edge
first, through the
machine. Feed the pasta
through six times more,
by which time it should
have become smooth
and silky in appearance.

If pasta is sticking, dust
lightly with a little flour.

Change setting on
machine to bring rollers
one notch closer
together. Feed pasta
through once only —
this will make the pasta
thinner and longer. Set
machine one notch
closer and again feed
pasta through. Repeat
this process to the
second thinnest setting
— at this stage the pasta
is the ideal thickness for
most uses. If you prefer
fine papery pasta, then
roll pasta through the
thinnest setting. Cut or
shape as desired.

CUTTING PASTA
Ribbon-shaped Noodles
Roll sheets of pasta
Swiss roll style to form a
long cylinder shape.
Slice into desired widths.
Unravel and cook
straight away or allow
pasta to dry in a warm
airy spot before storing.
If pasta is a little too
moist, dust it lightly

lling pasta by hand

*lace dough on a lightly
ured board and roll
m the centre outwards.*

*2 Roll until thin and use
as required.*

lling pasta with a machine

*eed flattened dough
ough rollers.*

2 Fold pasta into three.

*3 Feed pasta again
through rollers, reducing
width until thin.*

with flour before rolling. Rolled pasta can be fed through the cutters of a pasta machine to form long ribbons.

Lasagne or Cannelloni
Use a sharp, straight-edged knife or a sharp, fluted pastry wheel. Cut the lasagne to the same size as your lasagne dish or cut into sheets approximately 10 cm x 12 cm. Cut cannelloni into 10 cm x 12 cm sheets. These are then boiled and cooled before rolling around the filling.

Bows and Twists
To make bows: cut rolled pasta into 3 cm squares with a fluted cutter. Pinch two straight edges together to form bows.
To make twists: cut pasta into 5 cm x 2 cm lengths with a fluted pastry wheel. Cut a 2 cm slit down the top half of

the strip. Pull bottom half up through cut to form a twist.

Filled Pasta
To make tortellini: cut pasta into 5 cm rounds. Place a little filling on one side of round, and lightly brush half the edge with water. Join the moist and dry edges and press firmly together to form a crescent shape. Curve the crescent around and join tips together, sealing with a little water.
To make ravioli: place a sheet of rolled pasta onto a flat surface. Spoon mounds of filling across the width and down the length of the pasta at 4 cm intervals. Lightly brush between mounds with a little water. Lay a second sheet of pasta on the top of the first pasta layer. Press firmly between the

mounds. Cut between mounds into squares using a sharp knife or sharp fluted pastry wheel.

DRYING PASTA

Fresh pasta can be cooked as soon as it is made. However, if dri sufficiently, fresh past: can be stored in the cupboard indefinitely, ready for use when required.

To dry pasta shapes place on a flat tray line with absorbent paper on a wire rack, and pu in a dry airy place. Tu regularly until crisp an thoroughly dry.

To dry ribbon-shape noodles: either place loose nests of pasta on wire rack and leave to dry or hang pasta over broom handle or curta rod suspended betwee two chairs, and leave t dry.

Cutting pasta

1 Roll up pasta Swiss roll style.

2 Cut pasta into ribbon noodles.

3 Feed rolled pasta dough through cutting section of pasta machir

aping tortellini

Cut rolled dough into
unds.

Moisten half the edge
d fold over to form a
escent.

2 Spoon a little filling in
centre.

4 Curve crescent around
and join tips together.
Seal with water.

the pan. Boil until pasta
is *al dente* — firm yet
tender. Drain through a
colander or strainer and
if cooking water is milky
in appearance, then rinse
pasta with some fresh
hot or cold water (if the
cooking water is
clearish, this is
unnecessary).

To re-heat, place
pasta in a dish over a
saucepan of simmering
water for approximately
10 minutes or until
warm.

Other Types of Pasta
Instant or pre-cooked
lasagne and cannelloni
shells save time as you
can omit boiling the
pasta before layering or
filling. For best results,
soak the pasta in warm
water for 5–10 minutes
before using.

Pastas that contain a
filling such as ravioli or
tortellini are best
purchased fresh or
frozen. Fresh ravioli and
tortellini usually need to
be boiled 5–7 minutes
until tender. In frozen
form they need about 15
minutes cooking.

After pasta has
oroughly dried, store
an airtight container
til ready to use.
Commercial dried
sta is, of course,
adily available. It is
orth trying a few
fferent brands until
u find the one you are
ppy with, since brands
vary slightly in
xture and the time they
ke to cook.

OOKING PASTA
sta needs to be cooked
operly before serving.

esh Plain Pasta
his can be fried and,

for coffee treats, dusted
with icing sugar.
Mostly, however, pasta
is boiled in a large
amount of boiling water.
Traditionally salt is
added to the cooking
water. This is really not
necessary, as pasta has
plenty of flavour,
especially when
combined with delicious
sauces.

To cook pasta bring a
large pan of water to a
rapid boil. Add a little
oil to prevent sticking.
Add pasta and give it a
stir to ensure no pasta
has stuck to the base of

FLAVOURED PASTAS

You can add interest and variety to your pasta dishes by substituting fresh flavoured pasta for the dried commercial varieties. The possibilities are endless and it is worth trying a few different combinations:

Tomato Pasta
Add 1 tablespoon tomato paste and 1 clove crushed garlic (optional) to egg mixture. This pasta is a lovely rich orange which, during cooking, lightens a little.

Cheese and Basil Pasta
Add ½ cup finely grated parmesan and 2 tablespoons finely chopped fresh basil to flour before mixing with egg. Delicious served tossed with a little butter as an accompaniment to a meal.

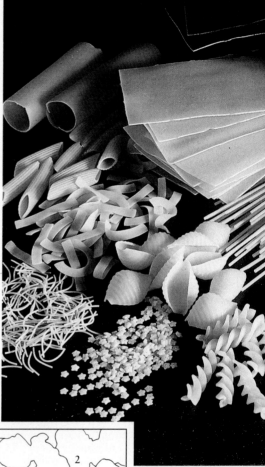

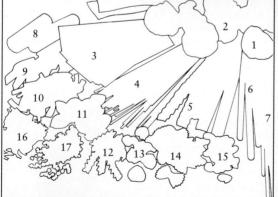

1. Fettuccine
2. Vermicelli
3. Lasagne
4. Spaghetti
5. Pappardelle
6. Rigatoni
7. Bucatini
8. Cannelloni
9. Penne
10. Tagliatelle
11. Shells
12. Fusilli

. Tortellini
. Farfalle
. Macaroni
. Gramigna
. Stellette

ickpea and Garlic
sta
place 1 cup plain flour
th chickpea flour, and
d ½ teaspoon garlic
wder to eggs. Best

served simply with a
little olive oil and
chopped fresh herbs or
chilli.

Lemon and Pepper Pasta
Add 2 teaspoons finely
grated lemon rind and 1
teaspoon coarsely
ground black pepper to
flour before mixing with
eggs. Delicious for

seafood-filled tortellini
or served with a light
cream sauce.

Spinach Pasta
Cook 225 g spinach
leaves until soft. Chop
finely and squeeze out
excess moisture to make
spinach quite dry. Add
to flour before adding
enough egg and oil to
form a dough. This
beautiful green pasta is
perfect for spinach
lasagne or as an
accompaniment to a
main meal.

Wholemeal Pasta
You can use all
wholemeal flour, but the
result can be a little
heavy. It is often best to
use half white and half
wholemeal flour. The
pasta may need a little
extra liquid depending
on the flour, in which
case use chilled water.
This pasta has a
delicious nutty flavour
and slightly heavier
texture than white
pasta.

Buckwheat Pasta
Replace 1 ½ cups of the
plain flour with 1 ½ cups
of buckwheat flour.

Almond Pasta
Combine 1 cup
wholemeal flour, 100 g
ground almonds, 3
tablespoons icing sugar.
Add 2 eggs and ¼
teaspoon almond
essence and mix to form
a dough.

9

–ESSENTIAL SAUCES–

Spaghetti with Fresh Tomato Sauce

Pasta is generally named after the shape, not the ingredients it contains. While some shaped pastas are more suited to particular styles of dishes, you shouldn't allow this to restrict you. Try different shapes for your favourite dishes and combine with any of these delicious sauces.

Rich Meat Sauce

With a stock of this in the refrigerator or freezer, you can make up many delicious recipes.

Preparation time: 30 minutes
Cooking time: 1¾ hours
Makes 1.5 litres

tablespoons oil
.5 kg minced steak
large onions, finely chopped
large green capsicums, diced
large cloves garlic, crushed
x 425 g cans whole tomatoes
cups tomato purée
x 235 g cans tomato paste
tablespoon dried oregano leaves
teaspoons dried basil leaves
½ teaspoon pepper
½ cups red wine
tablespoons beef stock

1 Heat oil in a large frying pan. Add meat a little at a time and brown, stirring constantly. As each batch is cooked, remove to a bowl. Repeat with remaining meat. Add onions, capsicums and garlic to pan and slowly cook until softened.
2 Return meat to pan with remaining ingredients. Simmer, uncovered, stirring frequently for about 1½ hours, or until thickened. Serve over hot noodles or sphagetti.

Anchovy and Garlic Sauce

Preparation time: 8 minutes
Cooking time: 5 minutes
Makes 1 cup

125 g butter
4 cloves garlic, crushed
2 x 45 g cans flat anchovy fillets, undrained and coarsely chopped
2–4 tablespoons hot water
1½ cups chopped fresh parsley
pinch pepper

1 Melt butter in a small frying pan. Add garlic and cook until tender.
2 Stir in anchovies with their oil. Add water and stir to mix. Add parsley and pepper to taste.

Serve sauce tossed through hot noodles.

> **HINT**
> The salty flavour of anchovies can be mellowed by soaking them in a little milk for 30 minutes before using. Drain and use as directed in recipe.

Tuna Sauce

Preparation time: 10 minutes
Cooking time: 15 minutes
Makes 2 cups

90 g butter
1 clove garlic, crushed
250 g small mushrooms, thickly sliced
¾ cup tomato purée
1 x 185 g can tuna, drained and flaked
pinch black pepper
chopped fresh parsley to garnish

1 Heat butter in pan. Gently fry garlic for 2 minutes then remove from pan. Add mushrooms and fry, stirring gently until just softened.
2 Stir in tomato purée, tuna and pepper to taste. Cook over low heat for about 10 minutes. Serve over hot noodles garnished with parsley.

11

Mushroom Cream Sauce

Preparation time: 10 minutes
Cooking time: 8 minutes
Makes 2 cups

60 g butter
185 g small mushrooms, sliced
1 clove garlic, crushed
300 mL cream
1 teaspoon grated lemon rind
pinch pepper
pinch nutmeg
3 tablespoons grated parmesan cheese

1 Melt butter in a pan. Add mushrooms and gently fry for 30 seconds. Add garlic, cream, lemon rind, pepper and nutmeg to taste.
2 Stir over low heat for 1–2 minutes. Add parmesan and cook gently for 3 minutes. Serve over any shaped macaroni or ribbon noodles.
Variation: Substitute crumbled blue vein cheese for parmesan cheese.

Fresh Tomato Sauce

Preparation time: 15 minutes
Cooking time: 45 minutes
Makes 4 cups

1 tablespoon oil
2 large onions, chopped
½ cup chopped celery
2 cloves garlic, crushed
4 cups chopped peeled tomatoes
½ teaspoon dried oregano leaves or 1½ teaspoons fresh
pinch black pepper
1 teaspoon sugar
1 bay leaf

1 Heat oil in a pan. Gently fry onions and celery until onions soften. Add garlic, tomatoes, oregano, pepper to taste, sugar and bay leaf.
2 Bring to the boil, lower heat, cover and simmer for about 40 minutes. Remove bay leaf and toss sauce through hot noodles to serve.

Variation:
If you wish, add 125 g small mushrooms about 10 minutes before cooking time is finished. Mushrooms can be quartered or sliced, then gently fried in a little butter and mixed through.

Pesto

Preparation time: 10 minutes
Cooking time: nil
Makes 1½ cups

125 g parmesan, romano or pecorino cheese, cut in small cubes
2 cloves garlic
½ cup pine nuts or walnuts
1 cup tightly packed fresh basil leaves
½ cup olive oil

1 Process cheese cubes in a food processor with chopping blade until finely grated. Add garlic, nuts and basil, and process again until finely chopped.
2 With machine running, slowly pour in oil through feed tube, processing until thickened and combined. Spoon over hot cooked and drained pasta. Toss well and serve.

HINT
Pesto is best made fresh when required. As fresh basil is not available all year round, pesto can be made using flat leaf parsley, which produces a different, yet delicious sauce.

Clockwise from top left: Mushroom Cream Sauce, Fresh Tomato Sauce, and Pesto

Tagliatelle con Prosciutto

See just how versatile pasta can be — there are so many delicious ways to combine pasta with fresh meat, chicken and smallgoods from the delicatessen. The recipes here can provide many memorable meals that will convert even the fussiest of your family to the delights of pasta.

These dishes are examples of both European and oriental cuisine, and are for the most part quick and easy to prepare. Try one the next time you want a deliciously different meal.

Tagliatelle con prosciutto

Preparation time: 15 minutes
Cooking time: 20 minutes
Serves 2

1 tablespoon oil
400 g tagliatelle
1 onion, sliced
30 g butter
200 g boiled ham, diced
150 g frozen peas
1 cup dry white wine
1 stock cube
½ cup water
2 tablespoons grated parmesan cheese

1 Bring a large pan of water and the oil to the boil. Add tagliatelle and cook for 6–8 minutes, or until firm and tender. Drain, rinse under warm water and drain again. Keep warm.
2 Heat butter in a pan. Fry onion until soft but not brown. Add ham and peas, and fry for a few minutes without browning. Pour wine over and cook until almost completely evaporated.
3 Crumble stock cube over top and add water. Bring to the boil. Add hot drained pasta. Serve topped with grated cheese.

> **HINT**
> To vary this dish, you can add 1 cup cream instead of the stock.

Spicy Tagliatelle

Preparation time: 15 minutes
Cooking time: 25 minutes
Serves 6

1 tablespoon oil
250 g each green and white tagliatelle
2 tablespoons chopped fresh parsley
4 tablespoons grated parmesan cheese

Sauce
30 g butter
1 onion, chopped
125 g peperoni or Hungarian salami, chopped
125 g button mushrooms, sliced
½ red capsicum, cut into thin strips
4 tablespoons dry white wine
3 tablespoons lemon juice
1 x 425 g can peeled tomatoes, chopped

1 To prepare pasta: bring a large pan of water and the oil to the boil. Add tagliatelle and cook in boiling water for 6–8 minutes, or until firm and tender. Drain, rinse under warm water and drain again. Keep warm.
2 To prepare sauce: melt butter in a frying pan. Sauté onion until soft. Add peperoni, mushrooms and capsicum. Sauté for a few minutes. Stir in wine, lemon juice and tomatoes. Bring to the boil. Reduce heat and simmer 5 minutes.
3 Return pasta to pan. Add parsley and parmesan. Toss well and serve immediately.

Oriental Beef and Noodles

Preparation time: 25 minutes
Cooking time: 30 minutes
Serves 4

1 tablespoon oil
500 g fettuccine

Sauce

4 tablespoons oil
500 g rump steak, cut into 2 cm cubes
1 onion, chopped
1 clove garlic, crushed
1 x 425 g can tomatoes, drained
2 tablespoons soy sauce
½ teaspoon finely chopped fresh ginger
½ cup beef stock
1 green capsicum, cut into short strips
1 tablespoon cornflour mixed with 2 tablespoons water

1 To prepare sauce: heat oil in a wok or frying pan. Brown meat a little at a time and transfer to a bowl. Add onion and garlic to pan,

Oriental Beef and Noodles (top) and Stir-fried Chicken (bottom)

irring well for 1–2
inutes.

Add drained tomatoes
nd cook for 5 minutes,
ressing tomatoes down
ith the back of a
poon. Return meat to
an. Stir in soy sauce,
inger and stock. Cover
nd simmer about 20
inutes or until meat is
nder.

Add capsicum and
pok for another 5
inutes. Add cornflour
iixture to pan and boil,
irring for another
iinute.

To prepare pasta:
ring a large pan of
vater and the oil to the
oil. Add fettuccine and
pok for 6–8 minutes, or
ntil firm and tender.
rain, rinse under warm
rater and drain again.
lace on a warm serving
latter and spoon over
ieat sauce.

HINT

To remove papery
coating from a clove
of garlic: crush the
clove under the flat
side of the blade of a
cook's knife. Peel
away papery coating.

Stir-fried Chicken

Preparation time: 25
  minutes
Cooking time: 20
  minutes
Serves 4

1 tablespoon vegetable
  oil
325 g Chinese noodles

Chicken and Vegetables
2 tablespoons vegetable
  oil
500 g boned skinned
  chicken, cut into 1 cm
  strips
2 thin slices peeled fresh
  ginger
dash bottled hot chilli
  sauce
4 cups prepared fresh
  mixed vegetables (e.g.
  carrots, tomatoes,
  broccoli, beans, snow
  peas or cabbage)
1 cup chicken stock
4 shallots, cut in 5 cm
  pieces
2 tablespoons soy sauce
2 tablespoons dry sherry
  or dry vermouth
1½ tablespoons
  cornflour
1 x 230 g can water
  chestnuts, drained

1 To prepare pasta:
bring a large pan of
water and the oil to the
boil. Add noodles and
cook in boiling water for
3–5 minutes, or until
firm and tender. Drain,
rinse under warm water
and drain again. Keep
warm.

2 To prepare chicken
and vegetables: heat oil
in a wok or large frying
pan until hot. Add
chicken, ginger and chilli
sauce to taste. Stir-fry
until chicken turns
white. Transfer with a
slotted spoon to a bowl.
Discard ginger.
3 Add vegetables to
wok and stir-fry for 3
minutes. Add stock and
cook 3 minutes. Return
chicken to wok. Reduce
heat and cover. Cook 3
minutes more.
4 Add shallots and cook
for 1 minute until
tender-crisp. Combine
soy sauce, sherry and
cornflour. Stir into wok
with water chestnuts.
Cook, stirring, until
thickened, clear and
boiling.
5 Spoon chicken
mixture over hot
noodles in a serving
bowl. Toss well and
serve at once.

HINT

Store fresh ginger in a
pot containing moist
sand. Slice off what
you require and
return remainder to
sand. This keeps the
ginger fresh and
moist.

Spaghetti and Meatballs

Preparation time: 25
minutes
Cooking time: 50
minutes
Serves 6

4 tablespoons oil
500 g spaghetti
grated parmesan cheese
to serve

Sauce
1 tablespoon oil
1 small onion, chopped
1 x 425 g can tomatoes
4 tablespoons tomato
  paste
½ cup water
½ cup dry red wine
1 small clove garlic,
  crushed
1 bay leaf
pinch black pepper

Meatballs
½ cup milk
1 cup soft breadcrumbs
500 g minced steak
1 small onion, very
  finely chopped
1 tablespoon grated
  parmesan cheese
1 egg, beaten
1 tablespoon chopped
  fresh parsley
pinch black pepper
¼ teaspoon dried
  oregano leaves

Spaghetti and Meatballs

To prepare sauce: heat oil in a pan. Add onion and fry until soft. Add remaining sauce ingredients and simmer for 20 minutes until thick, stirring occasionally.

2 To prepare meatballs: add milk to breadcrumbs and leave for 5 minutes. Combine soaked breadcrumbs with remaining meatball ingredients, mixing lightly but thoroughly. Form into balls and brown on all sides in 3 tablespoons hot oil. Add to sauce and simmer gently for about 15 minutes. Remove bay leaf.

3 To prepare pasta: bring a large pan of water and remaining 1 tablespoon of oil to the boil. Add spaghetti and cook for 10–12 minutes, or until firm and tender. Drain, rinse under warm water and drain again. Spoon meatballs and sauce over spaghetti and serve with grated parmesan cheese.

Chilli Pork and Penne

HINT
You can make soft breadcrumbs by processing bread slices in a food processor until crumbs form. Alternatively, grate stale bread on a fine wire cake rack.

Chilli Pork and Penne

Preparation time: 15
  minutes
Cooking time: 35
  minutes
Serves 4

1 tablespoon oil
350 g penne macaroni
parmesan cheese to serve

Sauce
150 g belly pork, cut
  into strips
1 onion, chopped
2 cloves garlic, crushed
½ fresh or dried chilli,
  or ½ teaspoon
  cayenne pepper
1 x 425 g can tomatoes,
  chopped

1 To prepare sauce: in a pan fry pork in its own fat until cooked through. Drain off excess fat. Add onion and garlic. Remove seeds from chilli and chop flesh finely. Add chilli and chopped tomatoes to pan. Simmer, uncovered, for 15–20 minutes.
2 To prepare pasta: bring a large pan of water and the oil to the boil. Add penne and cook for 10–12 minutes, or until firm and tender. Drain, rinse under warm water and drain again.
3 Place pasta on a warmed serving dish, top with sauce and a light sprinkling of parmesan cheese.

Beef and Macaroni (left) and Pasta and Quick Meat Sauce (right)

Beef and Macaroni

Preparation time: 25 minutes
Cooking time: 1½ hours
Serves 6

2 tablespoons oil
750 g round or topside steak, cut into 2 cm cubes
2 onions, sliced
1 clove garlic, crushed
¾ cup beef stock
2 sprigs fresh parsley
1 bay leaf
1 sprig thyme
1 cup tomato purée or juice
pinch black pepper
2 carrots, sliced
250 g rigati macaroni
chopped fresh parsley to garnish

1 Heat oil in a large pan. Add meat, onions and garlic, and fry until meat browns. Pour off excess oil from pan.
2 Add ¼ cup beef stock with the herbs tied together in a small bunch. Cover and cook gently for 30 minutes. Add half the remaining stock with the purée, pepper to taste and carrots. Stir well.
3 Cover pan and simmer for another 30 minutes. Stir in the last of the stock and bring to boiling point. Mix in pasta. Bring to the boil again, cover and cook 10 minutes.
4 Remove lid and continue cooking until pasta is quite tender. Remove herb bunch. Spoon beef and macaroni onto a serving dish and sprinkle with chopped parsley.

HINT
Partially frozen meat is much easier to cut into cubes or slices than defrosted or freshly sliced meat.

20

asta and Quick Meat Sauce

Preparation time: 15
  minutes
ooking time: 45
  minutes
erves 4

tablespoon oil
75 g spaghetti
rated parmesan cheese

auce
tablespoon oil
small onion, grated
clove garlic, crushed
00 g minced steak
2 teaspoon chopped
  fresh oregano leaves
  or ¼ teaspoon dried
x 37 g packet spaghetti
  sauce mix
¾ cups water
x 140 g can tomato
  paste
inch pepper

To prepare sauce:
eat oil in a pan. Add
nion, garlic and meat.
rown well over high
eat, breaking up with
e back of a spoon.
dd oregano, sauce mix,
ater, tomato paste and
epper to taste. Bring to
e boil, cover and
mmer for 15 minutes.
ncover and simmer for
nother 8–10 minutes.
To prepare pasta:
ring a large pan of
ater and the oil to the
oil. Add spaghetti and
ook for 10–12 minutes,
r until firm and tender.
rain, rinse under warm

water and drain again.
3 Place spaghetti on a
warm serving plate.
Spoon sauce over and
top with parmesan
cheese.

Beef Hotpot

Preparation time: 15
  minutes
Cooking time: 1 hour
  and 10 minutes
Serves 6

30 g butter
650 g lean beef mince
1 small onion, finely
  chopped
1 x 440 g can peeled
  tomatoes, chopped
2 stalks celery, sliced
200 g mushrooms, sliced
2 tablespoons tomato
  paste
3 teaspoons fresh
  oregano or basil leaves
  or 1 teaspoon dried
pinch black pepper

1½ cups water
1 small green capsicum,
  seeded and cut into
  short, wide strips
1 small red capsicum,
  seeded and cut into
  short, wide strips
500 g penne macaroni
4 tablespoons grated
  parmesan cheese

1 In a large frying pan,
melt butter and brown
mince and onion. Add
tomatoes with liquid,
celery, mushrooms,
tomato paste, oregano
and pepper to taste.
Cover and cook over
low heat for 20 minutes.
2 Stir in water,
capsicums and
macaroni; heat to
boiling. Turn mixture
into an 8-cup baking
dish and sprinkle with
cheese. Cover and bake
at 180°C for 40 minutes
or until macaroni and
meat are tender.

Beef Hotpot

Burmese Noodles

Burmese Noodles

*Preparation time: 30
   minutes*
*Cooking time: 20
   minutes*
Serves 4

*325 g Chinese egg
   noodles*

*1 double chicken breast,
   boned and skin
   removed*
3 tablespoons oil
3 onions, sliced
3 cloves garlic, crushed
2 tablespoons soy sauce
*1 stalk celery, thinly
   sliced*
*2 cups shredded white
   Chinese cabbage*

*500 g prawns, shelled
   and deveined*
pinch black pepper

1 Pour boiling water
over the noodles and
leave for 10 minutes.
Drop noodles into a
saucepan of boiling
water and cook for
about 3 minutes until

22

rm and tender. Drain,
read over two
icknesses of absorbent
aper on a wire cake
oler and set aside.

Cut chicken flesh into
ort strips. Heat oil in a
ok or frying pan. Add
nions and garlic, and
y until onions soften.
dd chicken strips and
y, stirring for 2–3
inutes. Stir in soy
uce. Cover and cook
ently until chicken is
nder. Mix in celery
nd cabbage and cook
nother 3–4 minutes.

Add prawns and
epper to taste and cook
r about 2 minutes,
ntil prawns are cooked
rough. Remove all
om pan and set aside to
eep hot. Add noodles
pan and toss gently
r about 3 minutes.
emove to a warm
rving platter and
oon the chicken
ixture over the top.

HINTS

☐ Bean sprouts,
snow peas and diced
ham are great
additions to Burmese
noodles.
☐ Sometimes this
dish is garnished with
scrambled eggs.
When ready to serve,
scramble 2–3 eggs in
the same pan until
firm, cut into strips
and scatter over the
top.

Spicy Pasta

Preparation time: 20
  minutes
Cooking time: 20
  minutes
Serves 6

1 tablespoon oil
500 g penne macaroni
grated parmesan cheese
  to serve (optional)

Sauce
1 tablespoon oil
1 large onion, sliced
1 clove garlic, crushed
2 cups sliced cabanossi
  (about 2 sticks)
4 mushrooms, sliced
1 x 400 g can artichokes,
  drained and halved
1 x 425 g can tomatoes,
  chopped
10 black olives, sliced
2 teaspoons chopped
  fresh chilli
½ teaspoon dried basil
  leaves
pinch black pepper

1 To prepare pasta:
bring a large pan of
water and a tablespoon
of oil to the boil. Add
pasta and cook in
boiling water for
minutes, or until firm
and tender. Drain, rinse
under warm water and
drain again. Keep warm.
2 To prepare sauce:
heat oil in a large frying
pan. Sauté onion and
garlic until onion
softens. Add cabanossi
and mushrooms. Cook
for 5 minutes. Stir in
remaining ingredients.
Simmer gently until
heated through. Add a
little water or red wine if
mixture becomes dry.
3 Place pasta on a
serving platter. Pour
over sauce. Toss to
combine. Serve with
salad and crusty bread.
Sprinkle pasta with a
little parmesan cheese if
desired.

Spicy Pasta

23

Chicken Balls in Tomato Sauce

Preparation time: 30 minutes
Cooking time: 45 minutes
Serves 6

5 tablespoons oil
500 g elbow macaroni

Chicken Balls
500 g chicken mince
2 onions, chopped
¼ teaspoon each dried oregano leaves and thyme
3 tablespoons dry breadcrumbs
1 egg, beaten

Sauce
1 onion, chopped
2 tomatoes, peeled and chopped
1 cup tomato purée
1 cup water
1 chicken stock cube
1 tablespoon red wine vinegar
1 teaspoon brown sugar
½ teaspoon chilli powder
pinch black pepper
2 teaspoons cornflour blended with 1 tablespoon cold water

1 To prepare chicken balls: combine all ingredients in a bowl. Mix well. Roll into walnut-sized balls between wet hands.
2 Heat 3 tablespoons oil in a large frying pan. Add balls a few at a time. Fry until golden. Drain on absorbent paper. Continue with remaining chicken balls. Set aside.
3 To prepare sauce: fry onion in 1 tablespoon oil until soft. Add remaining ingredients except cornflour mixture. Simmer for 10 minutes. Stir cornflour mixture into sauce. Bring to the boil, stirring constantly. Simmer for 3 minutes.
4 To prepare pasta: bring a large pan of water and 1 tablespoon oil to the boil. Add pasta and cook for 10 minutes, or until firm and tender. Drain, rinse under warm water and drain again. Spoon meatballs and sauce over pasta and serve immediately.

HINT
Meatballs can be successfully grilled or baked in the oven, rather than fried.

Chicken Balls in Tomato Sauce

—FABULOUS SEAFOOD PASTA—

Almost Instant Tagliatelle

Caviar, anchovies, fresh and canned fish, and seafood can all combine with many other flavours to produce exotic, delicious sauces, suitable to serve over a bowl of steaming hot pasta.

A sprinkling of fresh herbs and black pepper is often the best topping, since parmesan cheese doesn't usually lend itself to fishy pasta dishes.

Avoid long cooking of fish or seafood, as it becomes tough and very dry. It should only be just cooked, and served immediately.

Almost Instant Tagliatelle

Preparation time: 5 minutes
Cooking time: 8 minutes
Serves 4

1 tablespoon oil
350 g green tagliatelle noodles
1 x 185 g can tuna in brine, drained and flaked
90 g melted butter
4 tablespoons chopped fresh parsley
1 tablespoon chopped fresh mixed herbs or 1 teaspoon dried
2 cloves garlic, crushed
pinch black pepper

1 To prepare pasta: bring a large pan of water and the oil to the boil. Add tagliatelle and cook for 6–8 minutes, or until firm and tender. Drain, rinse under warm water and drain again.
2 Add remaining ingredients and toss through. Serve immediately in a heated dish.

Tagliatelle with Caviar

Preparation time: 10 minutes
Cooking time: 8 minutes
Serves 6

1 tablespoon oil
500 g green or white tagliatelle
90 g butter
pinch black pepper
1 x 300 mL carton sour cream
50 g black caviar
50 g red caviar

1 To prepare pasta: bring a large pan of water and the oil to the boil. Add tagliatelle and cook for 6–8 minutes, or until firm and tender. Drain, rinse under warm water and drain again. Add butter and pepper. Toss well.
2 To serve: arrange a portion of pasta on each plate. Top generously with sour cream and caviar.

Tagliatelle with Caviar

27

Pasta with Mussels

Preparation time: 25
  minutes
Cooking time: 30
  minutes
Serves 4

1 tablespoon oil
350 g bow-tie or shell-
  shaped macaroni
1 tablespoon sour cream
  (optional)

squeeze of lemon juice
crusty bread to serve

Sauce
1 kg fresh mussels in the
  shell
1 large brown onion,
  chopped
¾ cup dry red wine
2 tablespoons olive oil
30 g butter
125 g button
  mushrooms, sliced
2–3 cloves garlic,
  crushed

2 x 425 g cans tomatoes,
  chopped
1 tablespoon tomato
  paste
2 tablespoons chopped
  fresh basil leaves or
  2 teaspoons dried
2 tablespoons chopped
  fresh parsley
1 bay leaf, crushed
pinch pepper

1 Pull off hairy beards from mussels.

2 Simmer mussels, half the onion and
the wine for 5 minutes.

3 Add undrained tomatoes to mixture
and simmer until thickened to a sauce.

4 Combine cooked pasta with sauce
and reserved mussels, and heat through

1 Pull off the hairy beards from mussels and scrub shells well with a stiff brush under cold water to completely remove grit. Discard any mussels that have open shells or those which do not close when sharply tapped.

2 To prepare sauce: in a large saucepan, place mussels, half the onion and the wine. Heat until boiling. Reduce heat, cover and simmer for about 5 minutes until mussels open. Strain, reserving liquid. Discard any unopened shells. Set mussels and liquid aside.

3 In the same pan, heat oil and butter over moderate heat. Add remaining onion with the mushrooms and garlic. Cover and cook gently until onion softens. Add undrained tomatoes, reserved mussel liquid, tomato paste, basil, parsley, bay leaf and pepper to taste. Simmer, uncovered, stirring occasionally until thickened to a sauce.

4 To prepare pasta: bring a large pan of water and the oil to the boil. Add macaroni and cook for 8–10 minutes, or until firm and tender. Drain, rinse under warm water and drain again. Return to pan. Stir in thickened sauce and reserved mussels and heat through. Just before serving, stir in sour cream (if using) and lemon juice to taste. Serve with crusty bread.

Serve Pasta with Mussels piping hot.

Sicilian Spaghetti and Pasta Marinara

Sicilian Spaghetti

Preparation time: 10
  minutes
Cooking time: 17
  minutes
Serves 4

1 tablespoon oil
500 g spaghetti
3 tablespoons chopped
  fresh parsley
grated parmesan cheese
  to serve

Sauce
1 x 45 g can anchovy
  fillets
2 tablespoons olive oil
2 cloves garlic, crushed
2 tablespoons fine dry
  breadcrumbs
pinch black pepper

1 To prepare pasta:
bring a large pan of
water and the oil to the
boil. Add spaghetti and
cook for 10–12 minutes,
or until firm and tender.
Drain, rinse under warm
water and drain again.
Place in a warm serving
dish.
2 To prepare sauce:
drain anchovy fillets and
chop. Heat oil in a pan
and fry garlic until soft.
Add anchovies and
cook, stirring, for 2
minutes. Stir in
breadcrumbs and
pepper, and reheat.
3 Spoon sauce over
spaghetti and toss
lightly. Sprinkle with
plenty of chopped
parsley and serve grated

parmesan cheese
separately.

Pasta Marinara

Preparation time: 15
  minutes
Cooking time: 35
  minutes
Serves 4

1 tablespoon oil
350 g spaghetti

Sauce
1 tablespoon oil
2 onions, very finely
  chopped
2 cloves garlic, crushed

1 x 425 g can tomato purée
1 small carrot, coarsely grated
3 tablespoons chopped celery
1 cup red wine
1 teaspoon chopped fresh basil leaves or ½ teaspoon dried
pinch black pepper
1½ cups mixed uncooked seafood (e.g. prawns, mussels, scallops or crabmeat)

1 To prepare sauce: heat oil in a pan. Add onions and fry gently until soft. Add garlic and fry another 1–2 minutes. Add purée, carrot, celery and claret. Stir until boiling, reduce heat and simmer for 15 minutes.
2 To prepare pasta: bring a large pan of water and the oil to the boil. Add spaghetti and cook for 10–12 minutes, or until firm and tender. Drain, rinse under warm water and drain again. Place spaghetti in a warm serving dish.
3 To assemble: stir basil, pepper to taste and seafood through wine sauce. Reheat 1–2 minutes until seafood is cooked. Pour sauce over spaghetti and toss lightly.

Vermicelli Royale

Preparation time: 10 minutes
Cooking time: 12 minutes
Serves 2

1 tablespoon oil
225 g vermicelli (thin wheat spaghetti)

Sauce
1 cup cream
2 tablespoons chopped shallots or spring onions, white part only
pinch each paprika and pepper
60 g smoked salmon, cut into thin strips

Garnish
2 teaspoons salmon or red lumpfish caviar
fresh parsley sprigs

1 To prepare pasta: bring a large pan of water and the oil to the boil. Add vermicelli and cook for 4–5 minutes, or until firm and tender. Drain, rinse under warm water and drain again. Keep warm.
2 To prepare sauce: in a small pan, combine cream and shallots. Bring to the boil, reduce heat and simmer for 5 minutes. Stir in seasonings to taste.
3 Arrange pasta on warmed serving plates. Stir salmon into cream mixture and spoon over pasta. Garnish with caviar and parsley. Serve immediately.

Vermicelli Royale

Macaroni Pizza

Macaroni Pizza

Preparation time: 20
  minutes plus
  30 minutes soaking
  time
Cooking time: 50
  minutes
Serves 6

1 *tablespoon oil*
350 *g small elbow*
  macaroni
2 *x 45 g cans anchovies*
milk
185 *g Swiss cheese slices*
2 *tomatoes, sliced*
2 *teaspoons chopped*
  fresh basil leaves or
  1 teaspoon dried to
  garnish

Sauce
2 *tablespoons oil*
1 *onion, very finely*
  chopped
1 *clove garlic, crushed*
1 *x 425 g can peeled*
  tomatoes
1 *teaspoon chopped*
  fresh basil or ½
  teaspoon dried
1 *tablespoon tomato*
  paste

1 To prepare pasta:
bring a large pan of
water and the oil to the
boil. Add macaroni and
cook for 8–10 minutes,
or until firm and tender.
Drain, rinse under warm
water and drain again.
Drain anchovies. Soak in
a bowl of milk for 30
minutes then drain.
2 To prepare sauce:
heat oil in a pan. Gently
fry onion until golden.

Add garlic, undrained
chopped tomatoes, basil
and tomato paste. Cover
and simmer, stirring
occasionally, for about
20 minutes. Remove
from heat.
3 Grease a shallow
ovenproof dish about 25
x 28 cm. Spread half the
cooked macaroni over.
Spoon a layer of tomato
sauce over, cover with
rest of cooked macaroni.
Add cheese slices and
arrange anchovies in a
lattice pattern over the
top. Put a slice of
tomato in each lattice
square and sprinkle with
basil.
4 Bake at 190°C for
15–20 minutes, or until
heated through and
cheese has melted.

Bali-style Noodles

*Preparation time: 20
    minutes
Cooking time: 20
    minutes
Serves 6*

4 tablespoons vegetable
    oil
500 g capellini egg
    noodles
2 large onions, thinly
    sliced
2 stalks celery, thinly
    sliced
1 green capsicum, thinly
    sliced
1 red capsicum, thinly
    sliced
1–2 *hot chillies, thinly
    sliced*
3 *tablespoons soy sauce*
3 *tablespoons dry sherry
    or fish stock*
oil for deep-frying
2 *large onions, thinly
    sliced (extra)*
500 g *cooked prawns,
    shelled and deveined
    with tails intact*

1 To prepare pasta:
bring a large pan of
water and 1 tablespoon
oil to the boil. Add egg
noodles and cook for
4–5 minutes, or until
firm and tender. Drain,
rinse under warm water
and drain again. Keep
warm.

2 Heat remaining 3
tablespoons oil in a large
frying pan. Add
vegetables and cook,
tossing frequently, until
just tender. Add soy
sauce and dry sherry.
Spoon hot noodles over
and cook, tossing
constantly, until all
ingredients are
combined and heated.
3 Deep-fry the extra
onions in oil until
browned and crisp. Add
prawns and heat
through. Turn noodles
onto a heated platter,
and scatter prawns and
onions over the top.

Bali-style Noodles

–PASTA WITH CREAM AND CHEESE–

Fabulous pasta served with butter and cheese

The delicate flavours of fresh cheese, cream and milk combine deliciously with the stronger flavours of hard cheeses, to form pasta sauces that can be made in double quick time.

Enrich sauces with a little egg yolk or a dob of butter and a few seasonings, and you will produce a meal fit for a king.

Buttered Noodles

Preparation time: 5 minutes
Cooking time: 12 minutes
Serves 6

1 tablespoon oil
500 g fettuccine
60 g butter
1 cup cream
1 cup grated parmesan cheese
pinch black pepper

1 To prepare pasta: bring a large pan of water and the oil to the boil. Add fettuccine and cook for 6–8 minutes, or until firm and tender. Drain, rinse under warm water and drain again. Place in a warm serving bowl.
2 Melt butter in a pan over low heat. Mix in cream, parmesan and pepper, and heat gently. Pour butter mixture over pasta, toss well and serve at once.

Noodle Bake

Preparation time: 10 minutes
Cooking time: 35 minutes
Serves 6

2½ cups cooked egg noodles
1 cup cottage cheese
1 cup sour cream
½ cup sliced shallots
2 cups Rich Meat Sauce (see recipe on p.11)
snipped fresh chives
¾ cup coarsely grated cheddar cheese

1 Combine noodles, cottage cheese, sour cream and shallots. When thoroughly mixed, spoon into a greased shallow ovenproof dish.
2 Pour the meat sauce over, sprinkle lightly with chives and top with grated cheese. Bake at 180°C for about 35 minutes, or until heated through, and bubbling on top.

HINT
Fresh cream can be soured with the addition of 1 teaspoon vinegar per cup of cream.

Noodle Bake

Clockwise from left: Spaghetti Creole, Blue Cheese Tagliatelle, and Spaghetti Carbonara

Spaghetti Creole

Preparation time: 15
  minutes
Cooking time: 30
  minutes
Serves 6

1 tablespoon oil
500 g spaghetti

chopped fresh parsley to
  garnish

Sauce
60 g butter
500 g green prawns,
  shelled and deveined
100 mL white wine
1 x 425 g can peeled
  tomatoes, crushed
pinch black pepper

2 teaspoons curry
  powder
1 x 300 mL carton
  cream
2 tablespoons grated
  parmesan cheese

1 To prepare sauce:
melt butter in a frying
pan. Cook prawns until
just pink. Remove

rawns from pan and set
side. Add wine,
omatoes, seasonings,
cream and cheese.
immer for 10 minutes.
  To prepare pasta:
ring a large pan of
vater and the oil to the
oil. Add spaghetti and
ook for 10–12 minutes,
r until firm and tender.
Drain, rinse under warm
vater and drain again.
Return to pan. Add
rawn sauce. Toss over
ow heat for 1–2
ninutes. Serve garnished
vith parsley.

HINT
Devein green prawns
by cutting along the
back of the prawn
with a sharp knife
and removing vein.

paghetti
Carbonara

Preparation time: 10
  minutes
Cooking time: 15
  minutes
erves 6

tablespoon oil
00 g spaghetti
hopped fresh chives or
  parsley to garnish

auce
teaspoon butter
rashers rindless bacon,
  chopped
x 300 mL carton
  cream
egg yolks

2 tablespoons grated
  parmesan cheese
seasonings to taste

1 To prepare sauce:
heat butter in a pan.
Cook bacon until
brown. Add cream all at
once. Bring to the boil.
Reduce heat and simmer
for 2 minutes. Remove
from heat and stir in egg
yolks, cheese and
seasonings and set aside.
2 To prepare pasta:
bring a large pan of
water and the oil to the
boil. Add spaghetti and
cook for 10–12 minutes,
or until firm and tender.
Drain, rinse under warm
water and drain again.
3 Toss sauce through
pasta. Garnish with
chives. Serve on a warm
serving platter.

Blue Cheese
Tagliatelle

Preparation time: 10
  minutes
Cooking time: 20
  minutes
Serves 6

1 tablespoon oil
500 g white or green
  tagliatelle
2–3 tablespoons grated
  parmesan cheese

chopped fresh parsley to
  garnish

Sauce
30 g butter
2 zucchini, sliced
1 clove garlic, crushed
100 mL white wine
100 g blue cheese,
  crumbled
1 x 300 mL carton
  cream
pinch black pepper

1 To prepare sauce:
melt butter in a frying
pan. Cool zucchini and
garlic until zucchini is
tender. Stir in wine,
cheese, cream and
pepper to taste. Simmer
for 10 minutes.
2 To prepare pasta:
bring a large pan of
water and the oil to the
boil. Add tagliatelle and
cook for 6–8 minutes, or
until firm and tender.
Drain, rinse under warm
water and drain again.
3 Return pasta to pan.
Add sauce. Toss through
pasta for a few minutes
over low heat. Serve
sprinkled with parmesan
and parsley.

HINT
Fresh herbs give a
better flavour to
sauces, so where
possible, use fresh
rather than dried. Use
three times as much
fresh herbs as dried,
i.e. 1 teaspoon dried
herbs = 3 teaspoons
fresh.

Pasta, Eggs and Mushrooms

Pasta, Eggs and Mushrooms

Preparation time: 20
 minutes
Cooking time: 35
 minutes
Serves 4

1 *tablespoon oil*
350 g *small elbow*
 macaroni
1 *onion, sliced*

Sauce
45 g *butter*
2 *tablespoons plain flour*
1½ *cups milk*

pinch cayenne pepper
4 *tablespoons grated*
 tasty cheddar cheese
125 g *small mushrooms,*
 sliced
4 *hard-boiled eggs*
¾ *cup soft breadcrumbs*
60 g *melted butter*

1 To prepare pasta:
bring a large pan of
water and the oil to the
boil. Add macaroni and
onion and cook for 8–10
minutes, or until firm
and tender. Drain, rinse
under warm water and
drain again.
2 To prepare sauce:

melt butter in a pan.
Add flour and stir for
1–2 minutes. Add milk
and cook, stirring, until
boiling. Stir in pepper
and cheese, and simmer
for 1–2 minutes, or until
cheese melts. Quickly fry
the mushrooms in a little
butter until softened.
Mix drained macaroni
into the sauce with the
mushrooms.
3 To assemble: spoon
half the macaroni and
onion into a greased,
shallow ovenproof dish.
Halve the eggs
lengthways and arrange

over the top, cut-side down. Cover with remaining macaroni.
4 Toss breadcrumbs in melted butter until coated. Sprinkle over macaroni. Bake at 190°C for about 15 minutes, or until heated through.

> **HINT**
> If cayenne pepper is unavailable, use fresh chilli powder instead.

Spinach Gnocchi

Preparation time: 40 minutes
Cooking time: 45 minutes
Serves 4

Gnocchi are small savoury oval shapes originally called ravioli in Italy. Although they do not truly come under the label pasta, they figure largely on the pasta menus of Italian restaurants in Australia. They are usually made with potato and served with melted butter, grated cheese or sauces such as tomato, cream or chicken liver.

750 g fresh spinach or young silverbeet, cleaned, trimmed and very finely chopped
400 g ricotta cheese

Spinach Gnocchi

2 eggs
1 cup freshly grated parmesan cheese
pinch pepper
pinch ground nutmeg
a little plain flour for rolling
90 g butter, melted

1 Place spinach in a bowl with ricotta, eggs, half the parmesan cheese, pepper and nutmeg to taste. Mix well until blended.
2 With flour-dusted hands, shape spinach mixture into 5 cm balls; lightly coat with a little flour to prevent sticking. Set aside on greaseproof paper until needed.
3 Heat a large pan of water to boiling. Drop gnocchi 3–4 at a time into water. Simmer until they float to the surface. Remove with a slotted spoon and drain briefly.
4 Transfer gnocchi to a buttered shallow baking dish. Top with remaining parmesan cheese and drizzle with melted butter. Bake at 200°C for 15 minutes until browned.

> **HINT**
> When cooking gnocchi, ensure water is kept at simmering point only — rapidly boiling water can cause the gnocchi to disintegrate.

Noodle Shell Quiche (left) and Pasta with Broccoli (right)

Noodle Shell Quiche

Preparation time: 25 minutes
Cooking time: 45 minutes
Serves 4

325 g very thin spaghetti, broken into pieces
2 tablespoons oil
250 g rindless bacon, cut into 5 cm pieces
1 onion, chopped
4 eggs
1⅓ cups milk
125 g Swiss cheese, shredded
½ cup grated parmesan cheese
½ teaspoon dried basil leaves
¼ teaspoon pepper
generous pinch nutmeg

1 To prepare pasta: bring a large pan of water and 1 tablespoon of oil to the boil. Add spaghetti and cook for 6–8 minutes, or until firm and tender. Drain, rinse under cold water and drain again. Place into the base and sides of a buttered 25 cm quiche dish.
2 To assemble: fry bacon until crisp in remaining oil; drain and spoon onto noodle base. Sauté onion in bacon dripping for about 3 minutes. Sprinkle over bacon and pasta. Whisk eggs and milk together, stir in cheeses, basil, pepper and nutmeg to taste. Pour into dish.
3 Bake at 180°C for about 30 minutes until filling is set and shell begins to brown. Cool slightly before cutting into wedges to serve.

40

Pasta with Broccoli

Preparation time: 15 minutes
Cooking time: 20 minutes
Serves 6

1 tablespoon oil
500 g tagliatelle
3 cups broccoli florets
4 tablespoons sliced spring onions
250 g very small tomatoes, halved or quartered (optional)
3 tablespoons chopped fresh Continental parsley

Sauce
45 g butter
2 tablespoon plain flour
pinch pepper
1/4 teaspoon dried basil leaves
1/4 teaspoon dried oregano leaves
1 1/2 cups milk
250 g ricotta cheese
125 g mozzarella cheese, diced

1 To prepare sauce: melt butter in a pan. Add flour and seasonings, and cook for 2–3 minutes, stirring. Add milk and stir until boiling and thickened. Mix in cheeses, stirring over low heat until thoroughly combined.
2 To prepare pasta: bring a large pan of water and the oil to the boil. Add tagliatelle and cook for 6–8 minutes, or until firm and tender.

Drain.
3 Steam broccoli until crisp-tender, about 3–4 minutes.
4 Toss drained tagliatelle with broccoli, spring onions and tomatoes, if included. Spoon into a heated dish. Pour hot sauce over. Garnish with parsley. (If sauce is too thick, thin with milk or cream.)

Parsley Garlic Noodles

Preparation time: 20 minutes
Cooking time: 8 minutes
Serves 6

1 tablespoon oil
500 g fettuccine

Sauce
3 tablespoons white wine
3 slices thick white bread, crusts removed
1 cup chopped fresh parsley
3 cloves garlic, crushed
1/4 teaspoon black pepper
1/2 cup olive oil

1 To prepare sauce: sprinkle wine over bread and soak for 10 minutes, then break into pieces.
2 Combine parsley, garlic and pepper and gradually add olive oil. Add the bread, a little at a time, beating after each addition until mixture is smooth and thick. Set aside.
3 To prepare pasta: bring a large pan of water and the oil to the boil. Add fettuccine and cook for 6–8 minutes, or until firm and tender. Drain, rinse under warm water and drain again. Transfer pasta to a warm serving bowl, spoon sauce over hot pasta and toss to combine.

Parsley Garlic Noodles

–PASTA AND VEGETABLES–

Spaghetti Napoletana

Combine the versatility of pasta with the endless variety of vegetables and you have the basis of many delicious meals. The range of interesting combinations here will please the vegetarian and non vegetarian alike.

Spaghetti Napoletana

Preparation time: 20
  minutes
Cooking time: 20
  minutes
Serves 4

1 tablespoon oil
500 g spaghetti
grated parmesan or
  romano cheese to
  serve

Sauce
2 tablespoons oil
1 onion, sliced
2 cloves garlic, crushed
500 g tomatoes, peeled
  and coarsely chopped
1 teaspoon sugar
1 bay leaf
pinch black pepper
1 teaspoon chopped
  fresh basil leaves or
  ½ teaspoon dried

1 To prepare pasta:
bring a large pan of
water and the oil to the
boil. Add spaghetti and
cook for 10–12 minutes,
or until firm and tender.
Drain, rinse under warm
water and drain again.
Keep warm.

2 To prepare sauce:
heat oil in a pan. Fry
onion and garlic gently
until softened. Add
tomatoes, sugar, bay
leaf, and black pepper to
taste. Cover and simmer
until tomatoes are quite
soft. Stir in basil and
remove bay leaf.
3 Transfer spaghetti to
a warm serving bowl.
Pour the sauce over and
toss lightly. Serve cheese
separately.

Spaghetti with Spinach Sauce

Preparation time: 15
  minutes
Cooking time: 20
  minutes
Serves 4

1 tablespoon oil
500 g spaghetti

Sauce
1 tablespoon oil

3 cloves garlic, crushed
2 x 250 g packets frozen
  spinach, thawed and
  drained
90 g pine nuts or
  chopped walnuts
2 teaspoons dried basil
  leaves
½ cup grated parmesan
  cheese

1 To prepare pasta:
bring a large pan of
water and the oil to the
boil. Add spaghetti and
cook for 10–12 minutes,
or until firm and tender.
Drain, rinse under warm
water and drain again.
Keep warm.
2 To prepare sauce:
heat oil in a large frying
pan. Sauté garlic until
softened, stirring
regularly. Add spinach,
nuts, basil and cheese.
Cook for about 5
minutes until thoroughly
heated. Spoon sauce
over spaghetti and serve.

Spaghetti with Spinach Sauce

43

Ricotta Lasagne Swirls

Preparation time: 45 minutes
Cooking time: 1 hour
Serves 6

1 tablespoon vegetable oil
12 fluted-edged or plain lasagne noodles
500 g fresh spinach, washed and chopped or 1 x 250 g packet frozen spinach, thawed and very well drained
1½ cups ricotta cheese
250 g mozzarella cheese, shredded
1 large egg, lightly beaten
2 tablespoons grated parmesan cheese
¼ teaspoon ground nutmeg
¼ teaspoon pepper
60 g butter
250 g fresh small mushrooms, quartered
1 x 445 g can or jar Italian cooking sauce
½ cup red wine, beef or chicken stock
½ teaspoon dried oregano leaves
½ teaspoon dried basil leaves
chopped fresh parsley to garnish (optional)

Ricotta Lasagne Swirls (left) Macaroni Caprese (right

1 To prepare pasta: bring a large pan of water and the oil to the boil. Add lasagne noodles and cook for 10 minutes, or until firm and tender. Drain and rinse under cold water. Stand in a bowl of cold water.
2 Steam fresh spinach with a little simmering water in a covered pan for 5–7 minutes. Drain well. (If using thawed frozen spinach, drain well, squeezing out excess moisture with the back of a spoon.) In a bowl, combine spinach, ricotta, half the mozzarella, the egg, parmesan, nutmeg and pepper. Set mixture aside.
3 Melt butter in a pan. Sauté mushrooms over high heat until just wilted. Remove from heat and cool. Combine Italian cooking sauce, wine, oregano and basil. Spoon half the mixture into a baking dish. Lift noodles, one at a time, from water and drain on paper towels. Spread each with 3 tablespoons of cheese mixture. Place

An unusual Italian-style entrée — uncooked sauce is tossed through pasta.

1 tablespoon oil
500 g macaroni
125 g mozzarella cheese,
    cut into small squares
grated parmesan cheese
    to serve

Sauce
12 egg tomatoes or
    4 large tomatoes,
    thinly sliced
3 cloves garlic, crushed
1 red capsicum, thinly
    sliced
1 tablespoon chopped
    fresh basil leaves
½ cup olive oil
pinch black pepper

1 To prepare sauce: place tomatoes in bowl with garlic, capsicum, basil, olive oil and pepper to taste. Cover and leave at room temperature for 1 hour.
2 To prepare pasta: bring a large pan of water and the oil to the boil. Add macaroni and cook for 8–10 minutes, or until firm and tender. Drain, rinse under warm water and drain again. While pasta is still hot, add mozzarella, then the sauce, and toss together. Serve with a bowl of parmesan cheese to sprinkle on top.

3–4 mushroom quarters long each narrow end and roll up, Swiss-roll fashion, around mushrooms. Place, seam-side down, in prepared dish. Spoon remaining sauce over rolls. Cover dish with foil or a lid.
4 Bake at 180°C for 25 minutes. Remove foil and sprinkle with remaining mozzarella cheese and top centre of dish with any leftover mushrooms. Bake for about 5 minutes more, until cheese melts. Sprinkle top with chopped parsley, if desired, before serving.

Macaroni Caprese

Preparation time: 15
    minutes plus 1 hour
    standing time
Cooking time: 10
    minutes
Serves 6

—Fresh Pasta Salads—

Mediterranean Salad (left) and Macaroni Salad (right)

Pasta is delicious in salads. Combined with soft meats such as chicken or ham, or with crunchy vegetables, pasta's tender yet firm texture adds variety. The following recipes are perfect for summer nights on the verandah or entertaining with a barbecue.

Mediterranean Salad

Preparation time: 20 minutes
Cooking time: 10 minutes
Serves 6

Salad
tablespoons olive oil
500 g penne macaroni
small red capsicum, seeded and cut into fine strips
50 g peperoni, skinned and cut into julienne strips
tomato, coarsely chopped
cup shredded zucchini
1/4 cup shredded provolone or cheddar cheese
1/2 cup chopped fresh parsley
tablespoons pitted black olives
tablespoons finely chopped onion

Vinaigrette
4–5 tablespoons olive oil
1–2 tablespoons red wine vinegar

1 clove garlic, crushed
2 tablespoons chopped fresh basil leaves or 2 teaspoons dried
1/4 teaspoon dried oregano leaves
pinch black pepper

1 To prepare salad: bring a large pan of water and 1 tablespoon oil to the boil. Add macaroni and cook for 8–10 minutes, or until firm and tender. Drain, rinse under cold water and drain again. Transfer to a large bowl. Add remaining oil and toss well. Add remaining salad ingredients and toss lightly to mix.
2 To prepare vinaigrette: whisk together all ingredients, seasoning to taste. Pour over salad and toss. Cover and chill until served.

> ### HINT
> Capsicums are delicious with the skin removed. Cut in half lengthways, remove seeds and place under a hot grill until skin blisters and blackens. Rub off skin.

Macaroni Salad

Preparation time: 15 minutes
Cooking time: 10 minutes
Serves 4

1 tablespoon oil
325 g small shell macaroni
Italian dressing
1 x 440 g can four bean mix
1/2 cup sliced stuffed olives
4 stalks celery, sliced
1 white onion, grated
2 tablespoons chopped fresh parsley
mayonnaise (optional)

1 To prepare pasta: bring a large pan of water and the oil to the boil. Add macaroni and cook for 8–10 minutes, or until firm and tender. Drain, rinse under cold water and drain again. Transfer to a bowl, add enough Italian dressing to moisten and toss lightly.
2 Drain beans, rinse in cold water and drain again. Add olives, celery and onion. Sprinkle over a little more dressing and toss. Cover and chill. When ready to serve, sprinkle chopped parsley over the top and, if you wish, serve with mayonnaise or Italian dressing.

—DESSERT PASTAS—

Flambéed Bows in Orange Liqueur Cream Sauce

*T*raditionally pasta is considered a food *se*rved as a savoury dish, *bu*t this needn't always *be* the case. Here is a *se*lection of sweet pastas *bo*iled, baked or fried, to *te*mpt the fussiest taste *bu*ds.

*Where possible, avoid se*rving a pasta dessert *af*ter a pasta meal, as it *is* much too heavy. Pasta *de*sserts make a grand *fi*nale to a meal that is *lig*ht and simple.

*Fl*ambéed Bows in *O*range Liqueur *C*ream Sauce

*Pr*eparation time: 15 minutes
*C*ooking time: 10 minutes
*Se*rves 6

1 tablespoon oil
*5*00 g fresh pasta bows or twists
1 orange
1 lemon
*1*25 g butter
½ cup sugar
4 tablespoons custard powder
½ cup milk
2 tablespoons cream
3 tablespoons Irish Cream
3 tablespoons orange liqueur
*va*nilla ice-cream to serve

1 To prepare pasta: bring a large pan of water and the oil to the boil. Add bows and cook for 2–3 minutes, or until firm and tender. Drain, rinse under cold water and drain again.
2 To prepare sauce: grate orange and lemon zest. Finely squeeze juice and strain. Set aside. Melt butter in a large chafing dish, add sugar and citrus zest. Cook over low heat for 2–3 minutes. Stir in juice and bring to the boil. Blend custard powder, milk and cream together until smooth. Stir into orange sauce and return to the boil. Stir through pasta shapes and Irish Cream.
3 Pour in orange liqueur, warm lightly and ignite. Serve warm with a scoop of vanilla ice-cream.

Spiced Risone Pudding

Preparation time: 15 minutes
Cooking time: 50 minutes
Serves 6

125 g risone (see Note)
1½ cups milk
1 cup cream

4 tablespoons sugar
10 cm strip orange zest
1 cinnamon stick
½ teaspoon cardamom seeds
20 g butter
3 eggs, separated
½ cup caster sugar
2 teaspoons orange flower water
ice-cream or cream to serve

1 Place risone in a pan with milk, cream, sugar, zest, cinnamon and cardamom. Bring to the boil and simmer for 20–25 minutes until risone is tender and milk absorbed. Remove from heat, stir through butter and cool slightly.
2 Grease a shallow ovenproof dish. When mixture is cool, remove cinnamon stick and orange zest. Stir through egg yolks. Pour into dish and bake at 180°C for 20 minutes.
3 Beat egg whites until stiff. Gradually beat in sugar, a tablespoon at a time. Lastly beat in orange flower water. Pile egg white mixture on risone mixture. Return to oven and continue baking 5–10 minutes until meringue is golden and set. Serve warm with ice-cream or cream.
Note: risone is pasta that resembles rice in appearance. Available from delicatessens or large supermarkets.

Apple Cream Lasagne (below) Spiced Risone Pudding (above) (recipe on p. 53)

Apple Cream Lasagne

Preparation time: 40
   minutes
Cooking time: 40
   minutes
Serves 12

240 g instant lasagne
   noodles
vanilla ice-cream to
   serve

Apple Layer
1 x 740 g can pie apple
3 tablespoons brown
   sugar
2 teaspoons ground
   cinnamon
100 g pecans, roughly
   chopped

Cream Layer
250 g cream cheese,
   softened
3 tablespoons brown
   sugar
3 eggs

300 mL carton fresh
   cream
2 teaspoons vanilla
   essence

Crumble Topping
60 g butter
8 slices wholemeal
   bread, crumbed
½ cup sugar

1 Place lasagne noodle
in a large bowl. Cover
with warm water and

ak for 10 minutes.
rain.

To prepare apple
ayer: combine pie apple
with brown sugar and
innamon, mixing well
o break up apple into
mall pieces. Stir
hrough pecans. Set
side.

To make cream layer:
eat cream cheese with
ugar until light and
uffy. Beat in eggs,
cream and vanilla
ssence or purée all
ngredients in a food
rocessor. Set aside.

To make crumble
opping: melt butter in a
rypan. Stir through
readcrumbs and cook
or 2–3 minutes until
rowned and crispy.
Add sugar and cook a
urther minute. Cool
nixture.

To assemble: grease a
hallow lasagne dish
vell with butter. Spoon
alf the apple mixture
nto the base and cover
vith a sheet of lasagne.
pread over half the
cream mixture, top with
second lasagne sheet.
prinkle over half the
crumbs and again top
vith a sheet of lasagne.
Repeat apple and cream
ayers and sprinkle
emaining crumbs
irectly onto cream
ayer. Bake at 180°C for
5–40 minutes or until
rowned and golden.
tand 15 minutes before
erving. Serve warm
vith vanilla ice-cream.

Tropical Dip with Pasta Triangles

Preparation time: 25
  minutes
Cooking time: 10
  minutes
Serves 8

1 *quantity fresh Almond
  Pasta dough (see
  recipe on p.9)*
oil for deep-frying
*sifted icing sugar for
  sprinkling*

Dip
300 mL sour cream
pulp of 2 passionfruit
*1 x 440 g can crushed
  pineapple, drained*
*200 g white
  marshmallows,
  chopped*
1 cup shredded coconut

1 To prepare dip:
combine sour cream,
passionfruit, pineapple,
marshmallows and
coconut. Spoon into a
small serving bowl and
refrigerate for 1 hour.
2 To prepare pasta:
follow recipe directions
and roll out pasta on a
lightly floured board (or
through a pasta machine
to the second thinnest
setting). Cut pasta into
8 cm squares and cut
each square diagonally
across to form a triangle.
Heat oil to 190°C.
3 Deep-fry triangles a
few at a time until
golden and crispy. Drain
on absorbent paper.
Sprinkle liberally with
icing sugar. Serve dip
surrounded by fried
pasta.

Tropical Dip with Pasta Triangles

Pasta Stuffed with Spicy Nut Filling

Preparation time: 20 minutes
Cooking time: 45 minutes
Makes 15 filled shells

🖐

250 g large shell pasta
Crème à l'Anglaise to serve (see recipe)

Filling
125 g ground walnuts or pecans
125 g ground almonds
1½ cups cake crumbs
2 tablespoons sugar
¼ teaspoon ground cinnamon
¼ teaspoon ground nutmeg
½ teaspoon ground ginger
lightly beaten egg white to moisten
oil for deep-frying

1 To prepare pasta: bring a large pan of water to the boil. Add pasta shells and cook for 12–15 minutes, or until firm and tender. Drain, rinse under cold running water and drain thoroughly.
2 To prepare filling: combine walnuts, almonds, cake crumbs, sugar, cinnamon, nutmeg and ginger. Moisten with egg white until mixture is just holding together.
3 To assemble: take approximately 2 teaspoons of nut mixture and mould into each pasta shell. Press 2 filled shells together. Stand on a flat tray and chill, uncovered, for 30 minutes.
4 Heat oil to 190°C. Fry shells a few at a time for 3–5 minutes or until golden and crispy. Drain on absorbent paper and serve warm, with a little Crème à l'Anglaise.
Variation:
Dip cooled shells in melted chocolate to serve as petits fours.

Pasta Stuffed with Spicy Nut Filling

Crème à l'Anglaise

Preparation time: 10 minutes
Cooking time: 10 minutes
Makes 1¾ cups

½ cup cream
¾ cup milk
3 egg yolks
2 tablespoons sugar
3 teaspoons cornflour
2 tablespoons orange flavoured liqueur

Place cream and ½
cup milk in a pan and
bring to boil. Remove
from heat.

Beat together egg
yolks, sugar, cornflour
and remaining ¼ cup
milk until pale and
blended. Pour a little hot
milk into egg mixture
and combine. Add
mixture to pan and
blend.

Stir over moderate
heat until mixture boils
and thickens. Remove
from heat and stir in
liqueur. Cover with wet
greaseproof paper until
ready to serve.

Almond Tortellini with Fresh Fruit and Mascarpone

*Preparation time: 45
   minutes*
*Cooking time: 20
   minutes*
Serves 8

*500 g fresh mascarpone
   cheese*
300 mL sour cream
½ cup honey
*2 x 250 g punnet
   strawberries, washed
   and hulled*
*4 kiwi fruit, peeled and
   quartered*
*1 quantity fresh Almond
   Pasta dough (see recipe)*
1 egg white
50 g sugar
*2 cups desiccated
   coconut*
oil for deep-frying

1 Mix mascarpone with
sour cream and beat
thoroughly to combine.
Divide between six
individual serving dishes
and drizzle over 2
tablespoons honey.
Arrange fruit on
individual serving plates
and refrigerate until
chilled.
2 To prepare pasta:
follow recipe directions
and roll pasta out thinly.
Cut into 10 cm rounds.
Cover with a lightly
dampened cloth and set
aside. Whisk egg white

until stiff. Beat in sugar a
little at a time, until
shiny and glossy. Fold in
coconut and combine.
Spoon 2 teaspoons of
mixture on each round
of pasta. Brush half the
edge with a little water.
Fold in half and press
edges together to seal.
Heat oil to 190°C. Deep-
fry a few at a time for
3–5 minutes until golden
and crisp. Drain on
absorbent paper. Serve
warm on individual
plates with fresh fruit
and mascarpone.

Almond Tortellini with Fresh Fruit and Mascarpone

–PERFECT ACCOMPANIMENTS–

Clockwise from top left: a typical Antipasto Platter (all the ingredients shown are available from delicatessens), Italian Bread and Italian Style Salad

This chapter contains recipes for entrées, accompaniments and sweets, none of which contains pasta in their ingredients. They have been chosen from predominantly Italian dishes, because they go so well with pasta, complementing flavours and textures perfectly.

The addition of one of these to your pasta main course will help you to compose a perfect Italian meal.

The Antipasto Platter

Antipasto is the selection of hors d'oeuvres served at the beginning of the meal. The antipasto platter can be as simple or as elaborate as you wish to make it.

Italian delicatessens have a range of foods suitable to include on the antipasto platter with little or no preparation. These include:

*slices of salami sausage
olives
anchovies
ham
artichokes in oil
mushrooms or funghi in oil or vinegar
pimientos in oil
antipasto vegetables
thin slices of cheese
sun-dried tomatoes*

Figs and melon are also welcome additions and blend beautifully with thin slices of prosciutto or Parma ham, which is a raw salted ham served in paper-thin slices.

Other no-fuss additions include lightly fried eggplant, chunks of cucumber, cubed cooked potatoes, sliced raw onion, slices of fennel, radishes and hard-boiled eggs.

Fresh seafood served in olive oil and vinegar or with mayonnaise is also very popular and easy to prepare.

Arrange the platter so that you get an attractive contrast of colours and shapes.

Italian Style Salad

Preparation time: 10 minutes
Cooking time: nil
Serves 8

Salad
*¼ bunch endive
1 cos lettuce
1 radicchio or coral lettuce
1 fennel bulb, thinly sliced*

*1 x 250 g punnet cherry tomatoes, washed
1 red onion, thinly sliced
1 red capsicum, finely sliced
1 small cucumber, washed and thickly sliced*

Italian Dressing
*4 tablespoons lemon juice
4 tablespoons olive oil
1 clove garlic, crushed
1 teaspoon finely chopped fresh oregano leaves
½ teaspoon finely grated lemon rind
1 tablespoon parmesan cheese
¼ teaspoon black pepper*

1 Wash lettuce, endive and radicchio thoroughly. Separate leaves and arrange on a large shallow platter. Arrange fennel, tomatoes, onion, capsicum and cucumber on top of salad leaves.
2 To make dressing: combine all ingredients in a small bowl and whisk to combine.

HINT
Use any of the lovely salad greens in season to make this salad, including cos lettuce, butter lettuce, coral lettuce, sorrel and spinach.

Fresh Pears Poached in White Wine (left) and Zabaglione (right)

Fresh Pears Poached in White Wine

Preparation time: 15
   minutes
Cooking time: 20
   minutes
Serves 4

4 *ripe pears*
2 *cups water*

1 *cup white wine*
1 *cup sugar*
1 *cinnamon stick*
1 *strip lemon rind*

1 Peel pears leaving
stalk attached. Remove
core section with an
apple corer, leaving
pears intact.
2 Place water, wine,
sugar, cinnamon stick
and lemon rind in a large
pan. Bring to the boil.

Add pears and poach
gently for 5–10 minutes,
depending on ripeness of
pears. Pears should be
firm but tender when
tested with a skewer.
Lift pears out of liquid
with a slotted spoon. Set
aside.
3 Boil syrup rapidly for
5–10 minutes or until
slightly thickened.
Spoon over pears and
serve warm or chilled.

abaglione

reparation time: 10
  minutes
ooking time: 5 minutes
  erves 4

egg yolks
tablespoons caster
  sugar
cup marsala
ponge fingers to serve

Place egg yolks and
  ugar in a heat-proof
  owl. Whisk together
  ntil pale and creamy.
  tir in the marsala.
  Cook mixture over a
  an of simmering water,
  hisking constantly
  ith a balloon whisk or
  n electric hand beater.
  'hen mixture is thick
  nd frothy, pour
  nmediately into
  dividual glasses and
  rve with a sponge
  nger.
  'ote: it is important to
  ake zabaglione just
  fore serving, since the
  ooked mixture
  parates and becomes
  unny soon after
  ooking.

HINT
A beaten egg white
folded lightly through
the cooked
zabaglione makes it a
little less rich and
lighter in texture.

Lemon Water Ice

Preparation time: 20
  minutes plus freezing
  time
Cooking time: 5 minutes
Serves 6

This refreshing water ice
is characteristically icy in
texture, and makes the
ideal finish to a rich
meal.

600 mL water
⅔ cup crystal sugar
300 mL freshly squeezed
  lemon juice

1 Place water and sugar
in a pan and bring to the
boil over moderate heat.
Boil rapidly for 5
minutes. Remove from
heat and cool to room
temperature. Stir
through lemon juice and
place in the refrigerator
until chilled.
2 Transfer mixture to a
shallow metal tray and
place in the coldest part
of the freezer. Stir
mixture every 30
minutes until mixture is
frozen firm. Transfer to
a large container, cover
and store in the freezer
until needed.
3 To serve: spoon a
little lemon ice into
chilled glasses.

HINT
Scoop flesh out of
lemon halves after
juicing and fill lemon
shells with water ice.
Cover and store in the
freezer.

Lemon Water Ice

Italian Bread

Preparation time: 10
minutes
Cooking time: 10
minutes
Serves 6

*½ sheet focaccia bread
measuring
approximately
40 cm x 40 cm*
3 tablespoons olive oil
175 g butter, softened
4 fillets anchovies
4 cloves garlic, crushed
*3 tablespoons finely
chopped fresh basil
leaves*
*3 tablespoons finely
chopped fresh flat-leaf
parsley*
*1 teaspoon ground black
pepper*
*½ cup grated parmesan
cheese*

1 Slit bread horizontally
in half. Place cut side up
on a flat tray. Drizzle
both halves with olive oil.
2 Cream butter with
anchovies, garlic, basil,
parsley and black
pepper. Spread each side
of the bread with half
the butter. Sprinkle with
cheese.
3 Cook at 180°C for 10
minutes or until butter
and cheese melt and
brown lightly. Serve hot,
cut in squares.
Note: Focaccia is sold in
large flat sheets by the
quarter, half or whole. If
unavailable use 2 cm
slices of Italian bread.

Italian Bread

HINT
Continental parsley is
a flat-leaf variety,
which has a strong
distinct flavour.
Curly-leaved parsley
is an acceptable
substitute.

HINT
When chopping fresh
chillies, it is best to
use rubber gloves to
protect hands. If you
handle fresh chillies
with your hands,
avoid touching the
face or eyes, since
painful burning will
occur.

mond
Pasta, to make   9
Pasta Triangles with
    Tropical Dip   55, 55
Tortellini with Fresh Fruit
    and Mascarpone 57, 57
chovy
and Garlic Sauce   11
Sicilian Spaghetti   30, 30
tipasto Platter   58, 59
ple Cream Lasagne   54,
54

i-style Noodles   33, 33
sil
nd Cheese Pasta, to
    make   8
Pesto Sauce   12, 13
an and Macaroni
Salad   48, 49
ef
Hotpot   21, 21
nd Macaroni   20, 20
Meatballs with
    Spaghetti   18, 18
nd Noodles,
    Oriental   16, 16
Sauce, Quick   20, 21
Sauce, Rich   11
e Cheese Tagliatelle   36,
37
cconcini and Tomato with
Pasta   46, 46
ws
o make   6
Flambéed in Orange
    Liqueur Cream
    Sauce   52, 53
ead, Italian   58, 62, 62
occoli with Pasta   40, 41
catini   8
ckwheat Pasta, to
nake   9
rmese Noodles   22, 22
ttered Noodles   34, 34

banossi with Spicy
Pasta   23, 23

Cannelloni   6, 9
Caviar with Tagliatelli   27,
    27
Cheese and Basil Pasta, to
    make   8
Chicken
    Balls in Tomato
        Sauce   24, 24
    Pasta Salad Bowl   50, 51
    Stir-fried   16, 17
Chickpea and Garlic Pasta,
    to make   9
Chilli Pork and Penne 19, 19
Cream and Mushroom
    Sauce   12, 13
Crème à l'Anglaise   56

E

Eggs, Pasta and
    Mushrooms   38, 38

F

Farfalle   9
Fettuccine   8
    Buttered   34, 35
    with Parsley and
        Garlic   41, 41
Flambéed Bows in Orange
    Liqueur Cream Sauce   52,
    53
Frankfurters with Garden
    Pasta Salad   50
Fusilli   8
    with Potatoes and
        Spinach   46, 47

G

Garden Pasta Salad with
    Frankfurters   50
Garlic
    and Anchovy Sauce   11
    and Chickpea Pasta, to
        make   9
    and Parsley Noodles   41,
    41
Gnocchi, Spinach   39, 39
Gramigna   9

H

Ham and Pasta Salad   50,
    51

I

Ice, Lemon   61, 61
Italian Bread   58, 62, 62
Italian Style Salad   58, 59

L

Lasagne   8
    to make   6
    Apple Cream   54, 54
    Ricotta Swirls   44, 44
Lemon
    and Pepper Pasta, to
        make   9
    Water Ice   61, 61

M

Macaroni   9
    with Beef   20, 20
    Caprese   45, 45
    with Chicken Balls in
        Tomato Sauce   24, 24
    and Chicken Salad
        Bowl   50, 51
    Eggs and
        Mushrooms   38, 38
    Pizza   32, 32
    Salad   48, 49
    Tomato Bocconcini   46, 46
Meat Sauce
    Quick   20, 21
    Rich   11
Meatballs with
    Spaghetti   18, 18
Mediterranean Salad   48, 49
Mexican Pasta   47
Mille Righe with Tomato
    Bocconcini   46, 46
Mushroom Cream
    Sauce   12, 13
Mussels with Pasta   28, 29

N

Noodles
    Bake   35, 35
    Bali-style   33, 33
    with Beef, Oriental   16,
    16
    Burmese   22, 22
    Buttered   34, 34
    Parsley Garlic   41, 41
    Shell Quiche   40, 40
    with Stir-fried
        Chicken   16, 17

O

Orange Liqueur Sauce   53
Oriental Beef and
    Noodles   16, *16*

P

Pappardelle   *8*
Parsley Garlic Noodles 41, *41*
Pears Poached in White
    Wine   60, *60*
Penne   *8*
    Beef Hotpot   21, *21*
    Garden Salad with
        Frankfurters   50
    and Ham Salad   50, *51*
    with Pork, Chilli   19, *19*
    Salad, Mediterranean   48,
        49
    Spicy   23, *23*
Pepper and Lemon Pasta, to
    make   9
Pesto   12, *13*
Pizza, Macaroni   32, *32*
Pork and Penne, Chilli 19, *19*
Potato and Spinach with
    Spirals   46, 47
Prawns
    Noodles, Bali-style   33
    Spaghetti Creole   36, *36*
Prosciutto with
    Tagliatelle   *14*, 15

Q

Quiche, Noodle Shell 40, *40*

R

Ravioli, to make   6
Ricotta Lasagne Swirls   44,
    44
Rigati, Tomato
    Bocconcini   46, *46*
Rigatoni   9
Risone Pudding, Spiced   53,
    54

S

Salad
    Chicken Pasta Bowl   50,
        51
    Garden Pasta, with
        Frankfurters   50
    Ham and Pasta   50, *51*

Italian Style   *58*, 59
Macaroni   *48*, 49
Mediterranean   *48*, 49
Sauce
    Anchovy and Garlic   11
    Fresh Tomato   12, *13*
    Mushroom Cream   12,
        13
    Orange Liqueur   53
    Pesto   12, *13*
    Quick Meat   20, 21
    Rich Meat   11
    Spinach   43, *43*
    Tomato   24
    Tuna   11
Seafood Pasta
    Marinara   30, *30*
Semolina Pasta, to make   4
Shells   *8*
    Mexican   47
    with Mussels   28, *29*
    Stuffed with Spicy Nut
        Filling   56, *56*
Sicilian Spaghetti   30, *30*
Smoked Salmon Vermicelli
    Royale   31, *31*
Spaghetti   *8*
    with Broccoli   40, 41
    Carbonara   36, 37
    Creole   36, *36*
    Marinara   30, *30*
    and Meatballs   18, *18*
    Napoletana   42, 43
    Quiche   40, *40*
    and Quick Meat
        Sauce   20, 21
    Sicilian   30, *30*
    with Spinach Sauce   43,
        43
Spiced Risone Pudding   53,
    54
Spicy Pasta   23, *23*
Spinach
    Pasta, to make   9
    Gnocchi   39, *39*
    and Potatoes with
        Spirals   46, 47
    and Ricotta Lasagne
        Swirls   44, *44*
    Sauce with Spaghetti   43,
        43
Spirals
    Garden Salad with
        Frankfurters   50

with Potato and
    Spinach   46, 47
Stellette   9
Stir-fried Chicken   16, 17
Sweet Corn Mexican
    Pasta   47

T

Tagliatelle   *8*
    Blue Cheese   36, 37
    with Caviar   27, *27*
    Con Prosciutto   *14*, 15
    Spicy   15
    with Tuna, Almost
        Instant   26, 27
Tomato
    Pasta, to make   8
    Bocconcini with
        Pasta   46, *46*
    Macaroni Caprese   45,
    Sauce   24
    Sauce, Fresh   12, *13*
    Spaghetti Napoletana   4
        43
Tortellini   9
    to make   6, 7
    Almond, with Fresh Fruit
        and Mascarpone   57,
    Trevelle with Potatoes and
        Spinach   46, 47
Tropical Dip with Pasta
    Triangles   55, *55*
Tuna
    Sauce   11
    with Tagliatelle, Almost
        Instant   26, 27
Twists, to make   6

V

Vermicelli   *8*
    Royale   31, *31*

W

Wholemeal Pasta, to
    make   9

Z

Zabaglione   *60*, 61
Ziti
    Garden Salad with
        Frankfurters   50
    and Ham Salad   50, *51*